RED ROSES
FOR BRONZE

RED ROSES
FOR
BRONZE

By

H. D.

[Hilda Doolittle Aldington]

AMS PRESS
NEW YORK

Reprinted from the edition of 1931, London
First AMS EDITION published 1970
Manufactured in the United States of America

International Standard Book Number: 0-404-02145-X

Library of Congress Card Catalog Number: 72-119651

AMS PRESS, INC.
NEW YORK, N.Y. 10003

NOTE

I am particularly indebted to POETRY QUARTOS, RANDOM HOUSE for courtesy in allowing me to reprint *Red Roses for Bronze*.

The *Songs for Cyprus* were originally written for the play *Hippolytus Temporizes*, and appeared in that volume.

Other poems, here included, first appeared in A MISCELLANY OF AMERICAN POETRY, 1925 and 1926; IMAGIST ANTHOLOGY, 1930; POETRY, SATURDAY REVIEW OF LITERATURE, NEW REPUBLIC, Etc.

H. D.

Contents

RED ROSES FOR BRONZE

I

If I might take a weight of bronze
and sate
my wretched fingers
in ecstatic work,
if I might fashion
eyes and mouth and chin,
if I might take dark bronze
and hammer in
the line beneath your underlip
(the slightly mocking,
slightly cynical smile
you choose to wear)
if I might ease my fingers and my brain
with stroke,
stroke,
stroke,
stroke,
stroke at—something (stone, marble, intent,
    stable, materialized)
peace,
even magic sleep
might come again.

II

All very well
while all the others smirked,
to turn and smile :
you thought that I might see your joke,
would do
(fault of a better)
for the moment anyhow ;
you knew
that I would prove too strange, too proud,
for just the ordinary sort of come and go,
the little half-said thing,
the half-caught smile,
the subtle little sort of differentiating
between the thing that 's said
and that 's said not ;
the " have I seen you somewhere else ?
forgot ? impossible,"
the half-caught back half-smile,
the interrupted nod,
" a clod
may hold the rarest flower,
so I ? "
the question that 's an answer
and the thing
that means that what 's said
isn't answering ;
this,
this,
or this,
or this thing
or this other ;

the casual sort of homage that you care
to flick toward this
or this odd passing whim ;
the one above the second on the marble stair,
the smaller (or the taller) of those two,
chattering,
chattering
by the fountain-rim.

III

I count most men ignoble by your height,
neither too tall,
for some taste
none too slight,
but sensing underneath the garment seam
ripple and flash and gleam
of indrawn muscle
and of those more taut,
I feel that I must turn and tear and rip
the fine cloth
from the moulded thigh and hip,
force you to grasp my soul's sincerity,
and single out
me,
me,
something to challenge,
handle differently.

IV

I 'd say,
come let me start the thing at once,
to-day—
to-morrow will not do at all ;
I 've got a studio
near the Olympieum,
it 's cold in winter,
in summer—well
the heat
forbids an adequate comparison ;
they say discomfort
prods the ardent soul on ;
why must they vent on artists
all their venom ?
though that, of course, is all
beside the question—
I mean
come now,
to-day ;
forgive me ; your dark hair
catches the light
in serpent curves,
here,
there ;
that shimmer on the bay-leaf
where the sun
catches the bronze-green glint,
bay-leaf
or palm,
the sort of thing that spreads its ripple on

over across the helmets
to the stars ;

you might be Mars
or maybe Actaeon
the Huntress
bids her hounds
to leap upon.

V

I 'd hide my fervour in
" that sort of thing,
you know how tiresome it is,"
begin my mastery
in ironic wise,
making of mouth and eyes
a thing of mystery
and invidious lure,
so that all, seeing it, would stare,
so that all men (seeing it)
would forsake all women
(chattering)
I 'd make a thing at last,
downright,
not in the least
subtle
or insinuating ;

such is my jealousy and such my hate
though I would state it otherwise,
say ;
" as a favour,
just that turn of chin,
something I 've waited for,
you know the judges at the Pythian games,
the classic note,
the touch the world proclaims
perfection ;
tiresome ?

but I must finish what I have begun,
the tall god standing
where the race is run " ;

such is my jealousy
(that I discreetly veil
with just my smile)
that I would clear so fiery a space
that no mere woman's love could long endure ;
and I would set your bronze head in its place,
about the base,
my roses would endure,
while others,
those, for instance,
she might proffer,
standing by the stair,
or any tentative offers of white flowers
or others lesser purple at the leaf,
must fall and sift and pale
in (O so short a space)
to ashes and a little heap of dust.

IN THE RAIN

I

I said,
" the town bird
lifts a lordlier head,"
you said,
" the wild-swan only is kingly " ;
had I run less swiftly
across the square
(in the rain)
I had had breath to explain ;
I did not deign to stammer,
" but this,
but this—"
O kiss
that you did not give,
O name of tenderness
that you did not name.

II

I am glad ;
the cold is a cloak,
the gold on the wet stones
is a carpet laid ;
my hands clutch at the rain,
no pain in my heart
but gold,
gold,
gold
on my head,
a crown ;
while the rain pours down
and the gutters run,
(the lake is over-flowing
and sodden)
I say to myself,
" I am glad he never said good-bye
nor questioned me why
I was late."

III

I 'm late to-day,
you were late yesterday,
but he didn't say,
" I 'm sorry,
I kept you waiting,"
(the rain beats in my eyes again)
I lifted my face,
surprised
to see no answer in his,
no kiss,
(love is a trap,
a snare)
a bird
lifted a passionless wing ;
nothing,
nothing was ever so fair
as the wonder that clutched at me there,
unaware,
under the rain ;
my brain sang
a rhythm I never dreamt to sing,
" I will be gay and laugh and sing,
he is going away,"
I sang and sang under my breath,
" can death offer a sweeter thing ?
I am free ;
O pavements spread me your gold,
I am young,
I am young,
I am young
whom Love
had made old."

IV

I will be free,
no lover's kiss
to bind me to earth,
no bliss of love
to counteract
actual bliss,
(the wind,
the rain)
no pain of love
to cut the fibre of joy
that the wind is cold,
that the old, old streets
are beautiful
and the way to the temple,
that the court will yet be bountiful
with box-tree
and myrtle,
that the grove has recompense
of dedmet
and mehet-tree incense,
that some day
I will care :

then,
the air
will be full of multiple wings ;
the fountain-basin, bare
of ripple and circlet, will spring
into life,

will duplicate ring
on translucent ring
of amethyst water,
purple
and rare
crimson ;
the naked pillar will show
vermilion ;
in the empty square ;
the God will stand
with his bow
and intimate arrows ;
my heart will quiver and bow,
I will start,
remember
the touch of your hand on my brow,
(it was burning,
you healed it,
it was parched
and you cooled it)
but now,
I can walk by the shrine
and the sacred rows
of transplanted apples,
(Cydonian ?)
a barbarian,
an ignorant stranger
who knows
nothing of love.

V

Doves
circle and glitter and flare
wing and feather,
very-stars
of the upper air
(where Love is)
do I care ?
I seek sustenance
otherwhere ;
elsewhere
I find
shelter ;
I bind
the dark, dark fibre
of laurel ;
spite of you,
spite of all,
to spite
and in respite,
I will bow
to one God ;
(O intimate song,
my Lord,
O fire
and the Word) ;
I will leave
your personified things,
find strength
by an empty altar.

VI

Don't come there,
don't come,
you have all the world,
go anywhere,
everywhere,
you have cloak and wings and a rod,
all the paths are yours,
all, all the altars
save one,
this one
of my intimate God ;
don't come near,
go here,
there,
where you will,
you are Hermes,
Lord-of-the-dead,
you are a man,
feigning the godhead,
or a god pretending a man's weakness,
a man's wiles ;
frowning
or swift to smile,
you are a god above
and a god below,
Hermes,
treading the track of the dead ;
you said,
" you were late yesterday " ;
had a staunch heart bled

at a casual word
from a casual man ?
a god said,
" you were late " ;

you go to the under-world
or the gate of heaven,
while I tread
an earth,
devoid of your touch,
(unutterable bliss)
thank God,
devoid of your kiss.

VII

Your head
is bound with the myrtle,
is bound with the bay,
is bound with the red
rose ;
God knows
(being God)
why you stay with us,
why you trifle and traffic
and play
with us ;
if you lose,
if you gain,
do you care ?

a snare is Love,
a shame,
who are maimed with Love,
totter and falter and stare,
lost in a world
defamed,
bound round the ankles with violets,
with myrrh
and with half-opened myrrh,
trailing unutterable sweet
and lost,
lost,
lost ;
a wreck,

B

a circumscribed thing
is a man's heart,
touched by the wing
of immortal ecstasy,
we are maimed and weak,
and yet—

I was dead
and you woke me,
now you are gone,
I am dead.

IF YOU WILL LET ME SING

If you will let me sing,
That God will be
gracious to each of us,
who found his own wild Daphne
in a tree,
who set
on desolate plinth,
image
of Hyacinth.

CHOROS TRANSLATIONS
From *The Bacchae*

I

Who is there,
who is there in the road ?
who is there,
who is there in the street ?
back,
back, each to his house,
let no one,
no one speak ;
chasten your tongues ;
O cease
from murmuring,
for swift,
I cry with every note
of concentrated speech
my song to Dionysos.

O happy, happy each
man whom predestined fate
leads to the holy rite
of hill and mountain worship ;
O blessed, blessed spirit
who seeks the mountain goddess,
Cybele mother-spirit,
who carrying aloft
the thyrsus, ivy-wrapt,

waits upon
Dionysos.

Bacchantes,
swift,
be swift,
invoke and draw him back
from Phrygian mountain-peaks,
(God's son whom God begot)
back to the broad-paved
sacred towns
of Greece.

II

O Thebes,
Semele's nurse,
crown,
crown yourself
with pine branch,
with ivy
and the bright
fruit
of the flowering smilax ;
Thebes,
crown yourself with oak leaf
and dance,
dance,
dance
ecstatic ;
bind white wool
to the deer pelt,
lift high
the sacred narthex,
and dance until the earth dance ;
the earth must dance
when Bromios
conducts
his sacred high priests
from hill
to distant hill peak,
(those women whom the distaff
no longer claims
nor spun cloth)
driven mad,

mad,
mad
by Bacchus.

III

Ah, it is sweet on the hills,
to dance in sacred faun-pelt,
to dance until one falls faint,
to beat the sacred dance-beat
until one drops down
worn out ;
ah, it is sweet to rush
on, then,
to Phrygian hill-peaks,
to taste the sacred raw flesh
of mystic sacred goat-meat ;
ah, it is sweet,
ah, sweet
the Lydian hills with Bromios ;
Evoe,
Bromios leads us,
bearing aloft the narthex,
himself
even as the pine-torch,
himself the flame and torch-light,
cries,
on,
on,
on ;
the fields drip
honey
and wine
and white milk ;
the torches smell of incense ;
on,

on,
cries Bacchus, Bromios,
rousing the wandering wild pack,
enchanting them with glad shouts,
tossing his glorious hair loose ;
he chants,
he cries,
O, O forth
golden
as gold-decked Tmolos ;
Bacchantes,
beat deep drum-note,
with Phrygian chant,
sing Evius,
with sacred flute
and sweet note,
incite,
incite our wild dance
from hill
to distant hill-peak ;

so hearing him,
Bacchantes,
leap out
and as the wild-colt
at meadow,
round its mare's feet,
they beat
ecstatic dance-beat.

Strophe.   Again,
again in the night,
shall I beat white feet in delight
of the dance
to Dionysos?
shall I bear my throat to the night
air
and the dew in the night?
again shall my pulses beat
like the deer
escaped from the net,
from the knots
and the huntsman's shouts,
from the hounds
and the hunting riot?
shall I lie in the meadows sweet,
escaped,
escaped from the lot
of men,
like a faun in the desert,
like a wind
by the river bank?
again,
again
shall I rest
ecstatic in loneliness,
apart in the haunted forest,
hidden by leaf
and leaf-branch?

O which of the gifts of the gods
is the best gift ?
this,
this,
this,
this ;
escape
from the power of the hunting pack,
and to know that wisdom is best
and beauty
sheer holiness.

Antistrophe. Hard,
hard it is to wake the gods,
but once awake,
hard,
hard,
hard is the lot
of the ignorant man,
fanatic,
saying the gods are not ;
cunning,
cunning their nets,
hiding time's long, long tracks,
snaring the wretch ;
think not
by thought, to escape
predestined fate ;
it is so easy to know
wisdom is right,
easy,
easy to bow
to God in His might ;

doubt not,
rather accept ;
daemons have strength,
ritual is rooted in earth,
ancient and blest.

O which of the gifts of the gods
is the best gift ?
this,
this,
this,
this ;
escape
from the power of the hunting pack
and to know that wisdom is best
and beauty
sheer holiness.

Epode. Hope
has manifold power,
hope,
hope
has manifold face
to manifest men,
each different ;
some win,
some fail ;
happy, happy he
who, safe from the sea,
finds his sea-port
and home ;
happy, happy he

who rests,
when his work is done ;
happy the man of wealth,
happy of power,
but happier, happier far
I count
mysterious,
mystical happiness,
this one
who finds
day by day,
hour by hour,
mysterious,
mystical,
not to be spoken
bliss.

V

Strophe. Stalk,
stalk the prey,
away,
away to the hills,
hell-hounds of madness,
swift ;
leap toward the hideous freak,
this monster of wickedness,
track Pentheus down,
the clown,
mimic in woman's dress ;
on to the hills,
the rest
leave to his mother first,
leave to the dancing host,
let the wild Maenads press
toward him who would betray ;
hear,
hear his mother cry :
arise,
arise and slay
incarnate wickedness,
a godless man
and unjust ;
who, who has borne this beast,
no woman,
rather see
whelp of a desert lion
or Lybian Gorgoness ;
who,

who has dared appear ?
(hear,
hear his mother first,
spying him from the covert,
from the steep ledge of hillock)
hear,
hear,
O Bacchus,
see
who desecrates the hills ;
the hills belong to us,
invoke,
invoke
armed Justice ;
let Diké stand forth manifest,
let her step forth and slay,
slash him across the throat,
this monster,
Gorgon born,
Echion born
and born of earth.

VI

Agave. Take me,
my guardians,
where I shall look upon
no,
no,
no Cithaeron ;
my sisters and me,
one in our misery
shall re-invoke no old
passions and mysteries ;
the thyrsus shall pass on
to other Dionysians ;
O let me never see
haunted, mad Cithaeron
nor Cithaeron
see me.

CHANCE MEETING

I

Take from me something,
be it all too fine
and untranslatable and worthless
for your purpose,
take it,
it's mine;
no one can give as I give,
none can say,
" take bountifully and smile
and go away,
then, hate for ever;
do not stoop to send
the little missive
that might slay or end
this pain for ever."

Your one word might stay
the pain;
but do not send it;
keep yourself out of it,
intransient;
finish what you have begun,
write swiftly
with a stylus
dipped in sun
and tears
and blood,

rain,
hail
and snow ;
dip stylus in the beauty of the translatable
     things you know ;
the things I have
are nameless,
old and true ;
they may not be named ;
few may live and know.

II

Our hands that did not touch,
might have met once,
might just have gathered
this one in this one ;
impersonal fire, beyond us,
might have rushed
into our fingers ;
we 'd have known then
(being true)
one of the other ;
our hands might have crushed
red petal
of an island rose,
have done
with vanity of written word
and rhyme,
might have known once
(just in those fingers)
other leaves and stones,
touched Miletus,
known Samos,
lifted stones
from a small shelf
at Delos,
let grass slip
and seaweed,
(dead ten thousand years ago
that withers never)
in between our hands,
laughed
even ;

heaven is a near
translatable thing;
it's here,
it's there . . .

III

I thought my thought
might spoil your thought,
being fierce and rare,
holding bright points
as stars in the mid-air,
slaying and hating
that which it loves most,
even as the sun
the host of stars of night ;
even as the sun
must slay the stars
by day,
I thought my thought
would slay ;

I thought your thought
was rare,
made maps for men,
the words you write
are chart and rudder in a storm
or bright
as light-house,
set above the shoals ;

I thought your stars
must shine for men,
while mine,
must shine alone,

invisible,
to dominate me at noon
while others say,
" the stars are gone,
how odd to see
even a whisp of moon,
by day " ;
I say,
I thought that you might share my thought,
might cry,
" *the stars are shining,*
ringed about with the intolerable light
of the sun."

IV

Why did I think of others,
(being untrue)
say to myself,
" this one
and this,
and this
were wrecked by you,"
say,
" you have taken
ruthless and with power,
a burning glass
that concentrates ;
the fire,
once stolen,
you reject the ash,
you take the spirit,
let the body go,
to wander like the ghosts
Achilles knew " :

why did I hesitate ?
I heard a voice,
reiterate an oracle that gravely spoke :
" you took and did not give,
you praised and knew
the song they made was worthless
and the note,
they sung
was dross,

heavy and leaden by your silver-note,
the throat they lifted to bared winds
was slain
by voices in the wind ;
you heard,
they did not hear ;
you used them as the oracle, the seer
that speaks numb and unheeding what he says,
you bled them of their genius,
being dear
to oracle and altar of the Sun ;
we say,
you took whatever fire there was
and left them without love
and without power ;

desire crept to your knees,
you took it not to warm yourself
but to tempt near
the things that otherwise must perish
in the wind
and fire."

V

You didn't know
those Gods that pass,
those feet that come and go,
the parting of the curtain
where waves swell,
the holy sands,
the sunken holy well,
the wave that burns
and breaks a sharper blue
because for just one moment
some deft thought
severed the curtain
of that " then " and " now."

You thought as poets think,
suavely it 's true,
and you could turn
intricate river-runnels into words,
tell
wave-lengths in brave metres ;
all the same,
the spell
had passed you,
left you comfortless ;
you did not sense the wings beyond the gate ;
you could not see,
you could not touch and feel,
actually the sea-sand
and the sea-shell.

If you had caught my hand,
we would have dipped
our fingers
in any icy river,
sipped
a nectar
that had spoiled your life,
slain sister,
daughter,
mother,
friend and wife,
demanded headier loves
than your heart knew.

SEA-CHOROS

From *Hecuba*

Wind of the sea,
O where,
where,
where,
through the salt and spray,
do you bear me,
in misery ?
where,
where,
shall I be brought,
bought as a slave
for what house,
shall it be Thessaly ?
shall I wander along the creeks
where Apidanus breaks
myriad water-ways,
or sold
to some Doric sea-mart ?
O wind,
wind,
turn to me,
you who are swift to pace
beside the deep-sea ships,
who are swift to race
from crest to thundering sea-crest,
speak to me,
sea-wind,
hear ;

where,
where in the land of the Greek,
do you take me,
to what seaport,
exiled,
unfortunate ?

Wind of the sea,
O where,
where,
where,
through the salt and spray,
do you bear me
in misery ?
wind,
sea-wind,
shall it be
where first the bay and palm-tree
blossomed in mystic leaf,
sacrosanct to protect
fair Leto for the birth,
twin-born,
begot of High Zeus ?
wind,
wind,
shall I grow old
where the palm-trees still unfold
myrrh of leaf
and the laurel-tree ;
shall I sing,
chant in ecstasy,
with maidens, in the set dance,

gold arrows of the goddess,
her gold bow
and her head-dress ?
wind,
wind,
wind,
shall it be
that the sea-oars,
sweeping the sea,
take the roadway
to Delos ?

Wind of the sea,
O where,
where,
where,
through the salt and spray,
do you bear me
in misery ?
or nearer,
or further,
shall I
be claimed by another
and find
the shuttle,
the needle,
the loom
my fate ?
am I doomed
to the court
of far Pallas ?
what thread,

glowing crocus and red,
shall I thread
upon multiple thread,
till the pattern unfold
to depict
great Zeus,
son of ever-great Cronos?
shall I prick
out
the flight of the giants,
the fire-bolt,
Athena's yoked chariot?

Wind,
wind,
here I stand,
wind,
wind,
at an end;
Hymen has left me for Death;
love passes,
light passes
my hearth;
I face Europe
from Asia,
this lost land;
wind,
wind,
wind,
were it best
to die
in great Asia's death?

wind,
wind,
wind,
were it wise
to leave my children, my home,
my people (death's people)
to roam
afar
on the gathering wave-crests ?

Wind of the sea,
O where,
where,
where,
through the salt and spray,
do you bear me
in misery ?
or further,
or nearer,
I cry ;
I am lost,
I am dead
whether I
thread the shuttle for Pallas
or praise
the huntress,
the flower of my days
is stricken,
is broken,
is gone
with my fathers,
my child

and my home ;
wind,
wind,
we have found an end
in the sword of the Greek
and his fire-brand.

WINE BOWL

I will rise
from my troth
with the dead,
I will sweeten my cup
and my bread
with a gift ;
I will chisel a bowl for the wine,
for the white wine
and red ;
I will summon a Satyr to dance,
a Centaur,
a Nymph
and a Faun ;
I will picture
a warrior King,
a Giant,
a Naiad,
a Monster ;
I will cut round the rim of the crater,
some simple
familiar thing,
vine leaves
or the sea-swallow's wing ;
I will work at each separate part
till my mind is worn out
and my heart :
in my skull,
where the vision had birth,
will come wine,
would pour song

of the hot earth,
of the flower and the sweet
of the hill,
thyme,
meadow-plant,
grass-blade and sorrel ;
in my skull,
from which vision took flight,
will come wine
will pour song
of the cool night,
of the silver and blade of the moon,
of the star,
of the sun's kiss at mid-noon ;
I will challenge the reed-pipe
and stringed lyre,
to sing sweeter,
pipe wilder,
praise louder
the fragrance and sweet
of the wine-jar,
till each lover
must summon another,
to proffer a rose
where all flowers are,
in the depths of the exquisite crater ;
flower will fall upon flower
till the red shower
inflame all
with intimate fervour ;
till :
men who travel afar
will look up,

sensing grape
and hill-slope
in the cup ;
men who sleep by the wood
will arise,
hearing ripple and fall
of the tide,
being drawn by the spell of the sea ;
the bowl will ensnare and enchant
men who crouch by the hearth
till they want
but the riot of stars in the night ;
those who dwell far inland
will seek ships ;
the deep-sea fisher,
plying his nets,
will forsake them
for wheat-sheaves and loam ;
men who wander
will yearn for their home,
men at home
will depart.

I will rise
from my troth with the dead,
I will sweeten my cup
and my bread
with a gift ;
I will chisel a bowl for the wine,
for the white wine
and red.

TRANCE

The floor
of the temple
is bright
with the rain,
the porch and lintel,
each pillar,
plain
in its sheet of metal ;
silver,
silver flows
from the laughing Griffins ;
the snows of Pentelicus
show dross beside
the King of Enydicus
and his bride,
Lycidoë,
outlined in the torch's flare ;
beware, I say,
the loverless,
the sad,
the lost,
the comfortless ;
I care
only for happier things,
the bare, bare open court,
(geometric,
with circumspect wing)
the naked plinth,
the statue's rare,
intolerant grace ;

I am each of these,
I stare
till my eyes are a statue's eyes,
set in,
my eye-balls are glass,
my limbs marble,
my face fixed
in its marble mask ;
only the wind
now fresh from the sea,
flutters a fold,
then lets fall a fold
on my knee.

MYRTLE BOUGH

" I 'll wreathe my sword in a myrtle-bough."
HARMODIUS AND ARISTOGITON.

I

Your hands
make Pallas wonder,
yet your face
is dawn-spilled,
dew over
wild myrtle-flowers ;
strange dissonance—
intolerant eyes flare out,
steel glistens
on the field of desperate Mars ;
white myrtle and blue myrtle
and the sword,
wreathed with their tender stems,
Harmodius.

Then let me be a brother
to your need,
shoulder to steel-clad shoulder ;
let me take
the helmet
and the buckler
and the greaves, Aristogiton,
to your slender grace ;
let women fall beside us,
and men frown,

let us be soul and brother,
having won
the bitter wisdom
of Love's bitterest greed.

Love, beyond men and women;
having won
love beyond joy and sighing;
now be done,
O Perseus,
drop the Gorgon head, delay
your task
of making stones of men ;
having proved all your immaculate strength,
Harmodius,
be gone,
and hurl your armour and your greaves away,
tall,
feverish,
alert
Aristogiton.

II

And turn,
turn,
turn,
Narcissus,
from your reeds,
having stripped off
your weight of chastened, burnished armour,
see
your greaves
covered an ankle
wrought of goodlier stuff,
ivory ;
your chrysalis
of steel and silver
withers at the breath
of that wild thing it covers,
flower
whose scent
copies Assyrian odours,
while most sweet,
imperilled with the touch of Zephyrus,
it turns and shivers,
knowing its one bliss
to see itself,
itself,
itself
is this :

myself
who cast my silver-self afar,

armour and greaves and helmet,
for one star
rises above the sand-dunes,
one star lights
the pool above the marshes,
the fresh weeds ;
arise ;
delight
yourself in your own image,
Hesperus.

III

Yourself in myself,
mirror for a star,
star for a mirror,
water and wild, wild fervour,
some night-bird
crying to the impervious moon,
Cynthia
come soon,
Cynthia
come soon,
come soon :

see Love with Love is wedded for a day,
man with a maid ?
maid with a man ?
come, say—
are these two maids
or pages with bright shoon ?
O traitorous moon,
who hide your visage
in a starry veil,
woven of fire and blossom,
pause and tell
your secret to us
by this citron tree
that reaches skyward
to enchant your car,
tangling your axle
with its bloom ;

O star,
grant us the secret of your wanderings,
hold converse with us,
bid us to be wise ;
advise
Love whether Love is only man or maid,
or child or prince or god
or merely staid
warrior
with silver
bright
cuirass
for light.

IV

For you are armed
although you cast aside
your mounted gear,
helmet
and princely wear,
stamped with your rare
insignia of pride ;
nor can my manifold power
of song
and verse
and prayer
quell your stark will ;
you remain silver still ;
your flowers are not endangered
by my fever,
tall,
slender
and perverse young god,
Hermes
or Diomed,
or that one panting by the lapis water,
seeing alone the beauty
that must break
even his adamant heart
and make him kneel,
sensing at last the stark and perilous ache
that gods and mortals feel :

arise, O sleeping ivory,
and awake,

O open eyes
bluer than that blue lake
wherein you trace
each feature,
written clear ;
O fair and dear,
your stricken body
must die fretfully,
unless you rouse your marble self
and greet
your live self,
filled with fervour
in my face.

V

For you are graved indelibly
in each trait;
your mouth
is my mouth
and your throat,
my throat;
O dare the mouth,
sip nectar,
let the note
that brands and burns my utterance
be your song;
O feel as I feel,
brush your lips along
my eyelids,
open wide
beneath your frigid kisses;
let my pride sustain me,
passionless, rigid steel;
then having proved my inviolate strength,
support me,
let me reel,
nerveless and fragile,
fainting on slight stem,
toward you another wind-flower,
swept of rain;
two wind-flowers, loved of Cyprus,
two bright heads,
inscribed with the same script
that says
Adon
is dead;

or Hyacinth
has fled the earthly vale,
wan Hyacinth ;
let your bright slendour pale
as that one's did
before the fiery pain
and holy rapture
of his lord and king ;
so pitiful,
so beautifully adored
by him who left him on the wind-swept grass
crying alas,
again,
alas,
alas,
must all I touch
wither to nothingness ?

VI

For I must find
your vulnerable heel,
must burn and mark you
with a like rare steel
that burns and marks
each contour of my pride ;
how can you turn,
how can you think to hide
from Him
who struck great Helios,
who brought low
God ?
the eagle could not seek an eerier crag
but he must mock him
with a warier wing ;
God loosing Love
saw foot-holds unto hell
scarring remote Olympus,
and hell mocked
even high Zeus' most radiant palaces
when he delayed
bidding wan Orpheus sing ;

sing
and your hell is heaven,
your heaven less hell,
sing ;
let my own retarded rapture tell
you of the pulse,

the throb,
the quivering
that bade great Helios
drop the golden string
and spurn the lyre for ever ;
let song break
your icy cover,
O wild myrtle-frond,
wild myrtle grafted
with a Syrian bud,
bud of dark purple
in an ivory cup
of fragrant petal ;
O Tyrian shoot,
I would impregnate you
with sacredness
so that you never, never could be free
but loom
and waver
and waft terribly
white wings and wings of gold
across bright skies
be Eros to all eyes.

CHOROS SEQUENCE

From *Morpheus*

" Dream—dark-winged."

I

Give me your poppies,
poppies, one by one,
red poppies,
white ones,
red ones set by white ;
I 'm through with protestation ;
my delight
knows nothing of the mind
or argument ;
let me be done
with brain's intricacies ;
your insight
has driven deeper
than the lordliest tome
of Attic thought
or Cyrenian logic ;
O strange, dark Morpheus,
covering me with wings,
you give the subtle fruit
Odysseus scorned
that left his townsmen fainting on the sands,
you bring the siren note,
the lotus-land ;

O let me rest
at last,
at last,
at last ;
your touch is sweeter
than the touch of Death ;
O I am tired of measures
like deft oars ;
the beat and ringing
of majestic song ;
give me your poppies ;
I would like along
hot rocks, listening ;
still my ambition
that would rear and chafe
like chariot horses
waiting for the race ;
let me forget
the spears of Marathon.

II

Give me your poppies,
red with rarer white,
give me your just-unfolded
poppy-flowers ;
how strange—much longer
than a decade lost
is this one moment
when your breath is close ;
sustained,
held tense,
munificent strength delays
the ultimate profusion ;
long hours
trail in their purple
and long years are lost
in just this moment
while our souls are near,
our mouths separate ;
never another like this one
that holds our mouths asunder ;
hail and rain
and visible storm
and thunder
fled through the rocks
that our two beings made,
strong I
and you stronger ;
two crashing rocks ;
Charybdis
and that other,

ever twain,
apart,
ever sundered,
Scylla ;

give me your poppies
(new flowers spring from this)
fire breaks from Ætna
and a sheath of iris,
wild small dart-iris
and the headier sweet
(to heal us,
chill narcissus)
curl and drop
another offering
for your impetuous feet,
bull-throated god
or Pluto leaving Hell
for a white goddess.

III

I would forego
my snowfields for your sun,
I would surrender
crocus
and ice-gentian
and all the lilies
rising one by one,
one after one,
and then another one
like star that flames white fire
to star
as beacon ;
I would forget
the holy marjoram
and all the little speedwells
and low thrift
for just one grain
of your enchantment ; lift
the veil,
dividing me from me,
and heal the scar
my searing helmet made,
and lure me forth
radiant,
unafraid
as the immortals ;

we near heaven's hills with this,
God's asphodels ;

O stay,
stay close,
bend down ;
bend down my dream, my Morpheus,
breathe my soul
straight into you ;
I would revive the whole
of Ilium
and in sacred trance,
show Helen
who made Troy
a barren town.

IV

Again,
again,
again,
I would be done
with state and grandeur,
trailing through long rooms
in Tyrian colour
toward the Spartan throne ;
again,
again,
again,
I would strip off
the girdle
and the rare embroidery
of gold and silver ;
see, again I tear
the jewelled circlet
from my myrrh-bound hair ;
again,
again,
again,
I hear
the sea-wind raging
and again I seek
the sea-road leading
to the mightier sea ;
again
we round the sea-coast perilously ;
wind-beaten spume
and all the headier froth
conceal us

as we front the perilous north,
while Aphrodite's veil,
our talisman,
is lifted,
wafting us from dangerous shoal ;
again,
again,
again,
the blunt prow slips
over the sea-road
to your native land ;
warm sand
under my naked feet,
forgetfulness ;
then, sweet,
nothing but kisses
while the warriors shout
and Troy burns
and tall Greeks rush in and out
under charred gateways
back to weightier ships.

V

Phrygian and oriental,
now be gone,
Paris ;
and you,
you,
you,
give me your poppies,
O return to me
as if the very-god had come
straight from Euboea,
in his hand
a cone
of pine ;
I, mistress of the oft-imperilled zone,
translucent,
wrought of many colours,
step
ardent yet temperate
from my luminous throne ;
he smiles
and all the effrontery of all my race
rises to meet his smiling, cynical face,
and all my effrontery and all my wiles
blanch and wither
beside his enchanting smiles ;
and all the gold woven about my veil
and all the pearls, entwined
for their sorcery,
fail
beside the devouring embers

of his touch ;
I pale
beside him
who has vine and plant for dower,
I but a white rose,
one white rose
in flower ;

and Cyprus will not help me if I call,
for I am she
and she has chosen inimitably
(her way)
subtly,
subtle in mystery,
me for a while,
me for a vase, an urn, a thing for her only,
for her to prove
that men still live
and gods still deign
to love.

VI

Give me your poppies,
mightier, priestly state
must live with them;
Demeter at the gate
of hell,
awaiting springtime
and the host
of maidens chanting;
the Eleusinian coast
must flower again
with torch
and mystery;
the lost and lovely Daughter
must arise
and God must quicken hell
and Paradise
must be revealed to all;
give me your poppies,
let their radiance spill
rapture
for ever;
love me,
O love me,
never let me go;
beauty must spring
like violets out of snow
and children smile before us
as we pass
and faded loves
recall old happiness;

O give some poppies
to these lonelier ones,
let us not darken
all this luminous sun
with any thought
of jealousy or hate ;
O love, befriend this one
and this lost one ;
I shall not rate you for inconstancy ;
this flower is waiting for a little touch,
this one will wither in the casual blight
of sudden winter ;
give to the dead-alive,
the living dead ;
let them not mope in anger any more ;
O let them laugh and live
and praise God's ways
at once the hopeless ghosts
in ecstasy
murmured and gathered
(covering dazzled eyes)
to see the spread of wings
before hell's door,
the quivering
of Psyche's butterflies.

VII

So give me poppies,
nectar is less sweet;
this is no venomous fruit
nor poisonous leaf
but bread and wine
and lilies in broad cups;
O praise me dying,
lift me,
raise me up;
say I have loved you
in some holy wise;
say I have given more than woman could
and say you love me
as, in holy wood,
Orion bent
to shelter Artemis;
say I am wild and passionate
yet chaste;
kiss me
and say
you never kissed and never could again
a face so stricken in its rapturous pain;
now give me poppies,
drive the hurt away;
there is no unguent
of the Thracian vine
can give me half
you give,
no anodyne
from any Syrian orchard

can give more ;
my love,
the shore
even of sainted
distant holy Crete
lies spread like parchment
unrolled
at your feet ;

you waken all the sealed past
with your touch,
the hills of Ida
are the yellow sands ;
so shrive me,
grant the magic of your hands
as Paeon once, benignant, might have done
to one who died
of loving over-much.

VIII

So having died,
raise me again,
again ;
give me more poppies,
out of sleep, new flowers
rise fresh,
as rimming
river-wild Eurotas ;
give me more poppies ;
out of sleep and sleep,
the fringe of consciousness is lined with bright
wild,
wild,
wild,
wild,
white arums
and the night-lily,
feigning with narcotic breath,
the sacred peace
and holiness of death ;
give me more poppies'
scarlet, delicate bloom ;
kiss me ;
my room
merges with precinct
and the palace hall
seems to lend lustre
and ennoble
all,
all my trivial, simple little things ;

kiss me ;
the gloom
is edged with palpitant fire
where Love amazed
pauses in flight
to witness our desire,
for this, this, this
he sees
is something other,
mayhap (he thinks)
some potent visiting star,
flaming from aether,
from the middle-space
where Phoebus' horses
blaze their track
towards Dawn ;

how far,
how far,
a kiss may bear us
like a travelling ship ;
I slip
out of the borderland of consciousness,
kiss me again,
again.

IX

I live,
I live,
I live,
you give me that;
this gift of ecstasy
is rarer,
dearer
than any monstrous pearl
from tropic water;
I live,
I live,
I live,
I quaff a cup
that Lenaeus' happy troop
might stoop to offer,
skimming the surface of the purple vat
with wine-wreathed crater;
I live,
I live,
I live,
O hear
and champion him
you dear
and sainted Dryades,
grant him your dream,
ecstatic revelry;
reveal him to himself
as he himself to me,
who broke the clasp
to set the parchment free;

unroll before him too his hierarchy,
show him his gods from Asia,
his Assyrian
goddesses ;
define on parchment the bright sorcery,
outlined, with katha-flower
and martagon ;

hear,
hear,
you good and potent deities,
let him go free
of ancient superstition,
let him lift straight to sunlight
and bright skies,
as from the river-bed of Meroë,
the lotus lifts
its fiery passionate head.

X

I live,
I live,
I live,
you give me that ;
one grain of your beguilement
has more might
than all the contents
of Assyrian phials,
laid, by an Eastern magnate,
at the feet
of an enchanter
of the Median rites ;
I live,
I live,
I live,
O paragon,
who make the dead smile,
let me laugh again ;
give me a robe
such as I might have worn
below the sea,
cherishing the just-born
Achilles
with bright tales
and phantasies,
told in the same
monotonous little song,
like water going over and over and on,
on, on to mightier lakes
and stranger seas ;

let me forget the words that women say,
let me forget the very voice,
employ
water and wind
to tell the mystery
of love that comes to lovers being dead ;

O let me say the things
that Thetis said
to him when he had grown to lustihood
of warrior grandeur :
let me be the lover-mother,
lay again
your head here, here ;
there is no pain,
no disenchantment, no, nor evil spell
can ever touch you ;
see I tell
and tell and tell the same thing over again,
over and over
in monotonous tone,
I love you,
love you,
love you,
dear-my-own.

XI

Achilles stayed a moment and is gone,
man,
man,
and child,
the warrior,
all are one ;
I charmed the three
to unity in my arms,
I would re-make,
re-break them
and re-charm ;
go,
this perfection leads to ultimate death :
hemlock
(they say)
refines the deepest bliss ;
the night of ultimate darkness
waits us
who can fail
the quest,
the golden morrow
for a dream—slight
interim of madness ;
love,
this love I feel
craves anodine of hatred,
loneliness—fir and pine,
the crest of hill-tops,
scent of the wild cedar ;

I would be free,
be free ;
go
for I fear
lest I strike swift
as she, the lynx and bear ;
the Huntress claims me even amid the dream,
the breath of Artemis
stays this latter kiss.

XII

Medes,
Greeks
and Phrygians
suddenly are gone,
there is no lover,
no child
but a song;
song wrought enchantment,
said " you are a god,"
song made its sequence,
man
and man
and child;
now you have been a father to yourself,
let poppies wither
for this lovelier crown;
see,
I would pluck the olive
from my own
chaplet
to name you,
poet with the rest;
lover and lover,
man-child and a god,
all that is over;
see the kingly rod
is twined with laurel,
sacrosanct
and blest:

let us be gone,
remember what is best :
remembering this god last ;
though I was tired of measures like deft oars,
now I return,
a beggar,
crave far shores,
would take my place upon the rower's seat ;
avail myself of crumbs from hero's fare,
take lees of wine ;
steal, cringe,
slave with the rest,
only to beat time with them,
but to feel
intimately
of them, Argonites,
who scale
the Delphic head-land
on the Delphic quest.

XIII

Which
nevertheless,
through toil
and dreariness,
brings only bliss ;
which
nevertheless,
through pain
and definite loss,
brings only happiness,
alone
sanctity ;
His fiery kiss
must burn away this kiss
(this
and the one next after
and the next) ;
His fiery touch
must burn away the dross
of dreams of Medes and Grecians,
and the host,
flying with Helen,
and the frenzied troop
even of mad Iacchus ;
His ultimate kiss
alone must comfort us
who place love foremost,
then find song is best ;

love
is a garment

riven in the light
that rises from Parnassus,
showing
the night is over ;
see
He strikes,
as sunlight through a purple cloud,
and takes Love to him,
lover
and the shroud
of past endeavour.

HALCYON

" Bird—loved of sea-men."

I

I 'm not here,
everything 's vague, blurred everywhere,
then you are blown
into a room ;

the sea comes where a carpet
laid red and purple,
and where the edge showed marble,
there is seaweed ;

sedge breaks the wall
where the couch stands,
the hands of strange people,
twisting tassel and fringe

of rich cloth, become clear ;
I understand the people,
they aren't hateful but dear ;
over all

a shrill wind, clear sky ;
O why, why, why
am I fretful, insecure ;
why am I vague, unsure

until you are blown,
unexpected, small, quaint, unnoticeable,
a grey gull,
into a room.

II

You 're very dear,
but it isn't that,
there 's no rose and myrtle,
nothing, nothing at all,

only those small, small hands,
funny little gestures,
ways no one understands,
a figure under-small,

eyes that terrify people,
unfair estimates, prejudice,
hardly any charm,
yet that isn't everything,

that isn't by any means all;
a wind has started a little whirlpool
of sand where the carpet ought to be,
and shells lie

by the preposterous feet
of that woman who frets me, annihilates me,
O she will kill me yet,
my late cousin, the wool merchant's wife.

III

That 's life,
but I had grown accustomed
to disappointment,
insecurity, gloom ;

I begged for a place in their room,
I, a shadow, sought a place
where disgrace attended
the shape of a head-band wrong,

of a misplaced comb,
where reflected light
was caught in bowl and wall,
and silver all shimmering ;

" tinsel " they said the other lives were,
all those I loved,
I was forgot ;
O what, what, what

sent you, all grey, unnoticeable
and small
to shatter my peace,
unconscionable little gull ?

IV

Now the house shakes
(it 's in the very best suburb),
the town, the town-hall,
the agora, the market-stalls ;

the whole place is besieged
with a host of flying wings,
already they lie ruined—
all the consequent things,

and the rich, all those
whose place is with the best,
even the general's wife
and the pro-consul's widow

are reft of dignity ;
how can sand fly in hair
so carefully dyed
so rare a red ?

how can shells lie by sandals
so beautifully sewn
with cornelian
and Tryphlia-stone ?

V

Perhaps they said
when they sent you here,
" no one will see,
certainly no one will care,

an elf, no Grace,
an odd little castaway,
not fit for the gods yet " ;
we 'll let her drift

in and about the hulk
of the old world,
a dead place
and dull, beached, stranded

and thick with barnacle ;
O well, perhaps not ;
perhaps we were not
after all the terror and pain,

the curious betrayal,
the thousand and one things that people
  don't notice
(how could they ?)
forgot.

VI

You 're impatient, unkind,
lovers aren't that,
so it can't be love ;
you 're invariably blind,

bitter and crude to me,
cruel, whimsical ;
since you don't find
this colour agrees with you

(you say my dress
makes you sick)
go find some one else
there are plenty about ;

yes, I will shout,
don't say my voice displeases you,
nor my ways ;
O the days, the days

without these quarrels,
what were they ?
something like a desert apart
without hope of oasis

or a grot lacking water
or a bird with a broken wing
or some sort of withered Adon-garden,
O, one of all or any of all those things.

VII

Well then, never come again
since you found me out
the last time;
I can't stay in hour after hour

and wait;
you were late;
don't tell me over and over
about that dress,

purple, wine-colour,
with belt and shoulder straps
of grape and the over-
skirt with a long fringe

of silver; it's too late.
I have no lover nor want to be
taunted with age,
I'm too staid

for grape-colour,
for fringe and belt and straps
and ear-rings perhaps
and head-band of hammered silver;

I'm ill; I want to go away
where no one can come;
O little elf, leave me alone,
don't make me suffer again,

don't ask me to be slim and tall,
radiant and lovely
(that 's over)
and beautiful.

VIII

O for you,
because you 're a child—
now life will begin
all over again ;

and I thought
I was through ;
now I must be gay
where I was prim ;

now I must smile,
now I must laugh ;
(O, the grim, grim years)
O little, little gull,

let me put my head there
where the feathers turn from grey to white,
from white to grey,
and cry.

IX

You say, " lie still " ;
your hand is chill,
cold, unimpassioned,
inviolable ;

you say, " lie back,
you won't faint " ;
what makes you think that ?
what makes you think

I won't drift out,
get quite away ?
O, you know—you say,
" you can't now,

you must wait
to keep me alive,
for if you go,
I won't stay ;

I never had an illusion,
they hate me,
every one, every one,
but it 's worse for you,

you 're a baby, a lost star,
you never knew, nor saw,
you don't yet,
how horrible they all are."

X

No, it isn't true,
they 're not all horrible,
you 're always unfair ;
well there you see

we quarrel again—
don't talk—dismiss happiness,
unhappiness, pain, bliss,
even thought—

what 's left ?
incomparable beyond belief,
white stones,
immaculate sand,

the slow move-forward of the tide
on a shallow reef,
salt and dried weed,
the wind's low hiss ;

it 's here in my skull
(leave your hand there)
for you—for ever—
mysterious little gull.

SONGS FROM CYPRUS

I

Gather for festival,
bright weed and purple shell ;
make, on the holy sand,
pattern as one might make
who tread, with rose-red heel,
a measure
pleasureful ;

such as those songs we made
in rose and myrtle shade,
where rose and myrtle fell
(shell-petal or rose-shell),
on just such holy sand ;
ah, the song
musical ;

give me white rose and red ;
find me, in citron glade,
citron of precious weight ;
spread gold before her feet ;
ah, weave the citron flower ;
hail goddess,
beautiful.

II

White rose, O white,
white rose and honey-coloured,
tell me again,
tell me the thing she whispered ;

red rose, O wine,
fragrant, O subtly flavoured,
cyclamen stain,
how, how has your fire differed

from rose so white ?
swift, swift, O Eros-favoured,
part, meet, part—then
rose, be rose-white, unsevered.

III

Bring fluted asphodel,
take strip and bar of silver,
fling them before Love's shrine ;

see the white flowers turn red,
fragrance whereof the dead
breathe faintly by their river,

by Lethe's bank are rose,
and all the silver bars
shape to taut bows and arrows,

wherewith Love fronts his foes,
(ah, friend, beware his quiver)
wherewith Love fronts his foes.

IV

Where is the nightingale,
in what myrrh-wood and dim?
ah, let the night come back,
for we would conjure back
all that enchanted him,
   all that enchanted him.

Where is the bird of fire?
in what packed hedge or rose?
in what roofed ledge of flower?
no other creature knows
what magic lurks within,
   what magic lurks within.

Bird, bird, bird, bird, we cry,
hear, pity us in pain:
hearts break in the sunlight,
hearts break in daylight rain,
only night heals again,
   only night heals again.

V

Bring myrrh and myrtle bud,
bell of the snowy head
of the first asphodel;

frost of the citron flower,
petal on petal, white
wax of faint love-delight;

flower, flower and little head
of tiny meadow-floret,
white, where no bee has fed;

full of its honey yet
spilling its scented sweet;
spread them before her feet;

white citron, whitest rose,
(myrrh leaves, myrrh leaves enclose),
and the white violet.

VI

In Cyprus,
we sought lilies for her shrine,
(white and dark-petalled where Adonis bled)
but, here in Greece,
for one white lilies,
for another red,
nor any peace.

In Cyprus,
we nursed love within our hearts,
and sang and with the song we wove the dance,
but here in Greece,
love is a torment
and they drive him out, far out,
and sue for peace.

In Cyprus,
peace is not where love has left ;
I do not understand
the ways that seek white lilies for one love,
(casting aside the darker
scarred with fire)
and for another, red.

All flowers are hers
who rules the immeasurate seas,
in Cyprus, purple and white lilies tall ;
how were it other ?
there is no escape
from her who nurtures,
who imperils all.

LET ZEUS RECORD

I

I say, I am quite done,
quite done with this;
you smile your calm
inveterate chill smile

and light steps back;
intolerate loveliness
smiles at the ranks
of obdurate bitterness;

you smile with keen
chiselled and frigid lips;
it seems no evil
ever could have been;

so, on the Parthenon,
like splendour keeps
peril at bay,
facing inviolate dawn.

II

Men cannot mar you,
women cannot break
your innate strength,
your stark autocracy ;

still I will make no plea
for this slight verse ;
it outlines simply
Love's authority :

but pardon this,
that in these luminous days,
I re-invoke the dark
to frame your praise ;

as one to make a bright room
seem more bright,
stares out deliberate
into Cerberus-night.

III

Sometimes I chide the manner of your dress ;
I want all men to see the grace of you ;
I mock your pace, your body's insolence,
thinking that all should praise, while obstinate
you still insist your beauty's gold is clay :

I chide you that you stand not forth entire,
set on bright plinth, intolerably desired ;
yet I in turn will cheat, will thwart your whim,
I 'll break my thought, weld it to fit your measure
as one who sets a statue on a height
to show where Hyacinth or Pan have been.

IV

When blight lay and the Persian like a scar,
and death was heavy on Athens, plague and war,
you gave me this bright garment and this ring ;

I who still kept of wisdom's meagre store
a few rare songs and some philosophising,
offered you these for I had nothing more ;

that which both Athens and the Persian mocked
you took, as a cold famished bird takes grain,
blown inland through darkness and withering rain.

V

Would you prefer myrrh-flower or cyclamen ?
I have them, I could spread them out again ;
but now for this stark moment while Love breathes
his tentative breath, as dying, yet still lives,
wait as that time you waited tense with me :

others shall love when Athens lives again,
you waited in the agonies of war ;
others will praise when all the host proclaims
Athens the perfect ; you, when Athens lost,
stood by her ; when the dark perfidious host
turned, it was you who pled for her with death.

VI

Stars wheel in purple, yours is not so rare
as Hesperus, nor yet so great a star
as bright Aldebaran or Sirius,
nor yet the stained and brilliant one of War;

stars turn in purple, glorious to the sight;
yours is not gracious as the Pleiads' are
nor as Orion's sapphires, luminous;

yet disenchanted, cold, imperious face,
when all the others, blighted, reel and fall,
your star, steel-set, keeps lone and frigid tryst
to freighted ships, baffled in wind and blast.

VII

None watched with me
who watched his fluttering breath,
none brought white roses,
none the roses red ;

many had loved,
had sought him luminous,
when he was blithe
and purple draped his bed ;

yet when Love fell
struck down with plague and war,
you lay white myrrh-buds
on the darkened lintel ;

you fastened blossom
to the smitten sill ;
let Zeus record this,
daring Death to mar.

WHITE ROSE

White rose,
white rose,
white rose
that mocked the fire
of jasemine
and of lily
and of faint
pulse of the violet,
drained of purple fire,
(white violet,
you are no flower at all)
white rose
you are a stricken weary thing,
shaming the spring . . .

> *(ah hear him,*
> *hear him,*
> *hear him,*
> *let him sing !)*

. . . white rose
your wisdom is a simple thing,
and must we grieve who found you very fair?
white rose,
white rose,
beware,
beauty is beauty
but not, not so rare
and not so bountiful
that it may spare

a moment
to revile
Love ;
a moment to repent
once Love is fled . . .

>   *(see spring is gone,*
>   *ah wail, ah wail in vain,*
>   *for spring is dead,*
>   *Love having kissed the mouth,*
>   *the mouth*
>   *of youth*
>   *again !)*

CALLIOPE

" And thou thyself, Calliope."—SAPPHO.

To climb the intricate heights
of unimpeded rapture,
is no slight
task, O my love ;
yet rapture, the very loveliest,
changes,
inbreeds
blackest despair,
succeeds pure fire,
if you neglect
(as you neglect)
others ;
come back ;
spirit must not tempt flesh—

    Nor dark flesh spirit,
    nay, I am gone,
    gone out, out, out from this ;
    what holds me ?
    fervid, torturing, your kiss ?
    is love enough ?
    the intolerable host
    and throng of mortals spoil
    at last,
    even the most abiding, intimate
    bliss ;
    intolerable stain ;
    hate of the listless

unadoring host;
nay, I am out and lost.

O spirit, white,
and versed in mystic lore,
beware,
too soon, too soon
you think yourself exempt
from all our lower thought,
our lesser magic,
Love's exquisite revel;
grow not too soon, too bold,
return,
O sweet, bright Lydian,
loveliest,
O lily-cold.

Nay,
cheat me not with time,
with the dull ache of flesh,
for all flesh turns,
even the loveliest
ankle and frail thigh,
to bitterest dust,
I would be off;
I long for the white throng,
the host of the immortals;
nay,
fondle me not,
I must
break from your trammels—

Your wings,
O sweet, O sweet,
are not yet grown,
what were you
mid the great, eternal host·?
a beggar lost;
what were you
without shield of valorous flesh?
mine, mine;
my song it is that aches
to set you free;
my verse would break
the fleshly portal down;
I, I it is
that tends and spares your light,
lamp sheltering—

Nay, I am gone,
what is your flesh to me?
what is your chant, your sorg?
mid the immortals
all, as stars, swing free
and need no lamp of silver work or bronze;
I would escape;
in the high portals
of imperial Zeus,
no veils of baser flesh
chafe at us grievously,
see—
I am gone.

ALL MOUNTAINS

" Give me all mountains."
HYMN TO ARTEMIS.

Give me all mountains :
city,
town,
the precinct
of temple,
the crowded town-gate,
I have no love for :
walls must crush or hide
whether of market,
palace court
or precinct :
give me the streams cold path,
the grove of pine,
for garden terrace
the unclaimed,
bleak
wild stretches
of the mountain side.

Give me no earth,
crushed flat
with crude layer
of fitted square
or meted length,
but boulders
unhewn
and set apart

as secret altars,
high in the loveliest
alder grove
or poplar ;
give me for altar fire
the wild azalia ;
let Phoebus keep
the fervid market place.

Give him white marble,
him the luminous white
of sheltering porch,
carved pillar,
portico ;
give him the wharf,
the quay,
the street,
the market,
street corner
and the corner of the street ;
nor do I envy him
my fiery brother,
who count as fair
only the reach of snow,
set stark
in mid air.

Marble of islands,
snow of distant points,
threatened with wave of pine,
with wash of alder ;
my islands
shift and change,

now here, now there,
dazzling,
white,
granite,
silver
in blue aether ;
I swim
who tread the mountain path as air.

Let Phoebus keep the market,
let white Love
claim all the islands
of seaport or river
would I contend with these ?
nay,
I would rather pity him, my brother,
pity white passionate Love
who only knows
the promptings
of the restless, thwarted seas,
(shivering in porches
from the bitter air) ;
ah Zeus,
ennoble,
shelter these
thy children,
but give me the islands of the upper air,
all mountains
and the towering mountain trees.

TRIPLEX

A Prayer

Let them not war in me,
these three ;
Saviour-of-cities,
Flower-of-destiny
and she,
Twinborn-with-Phoebus,
fending gallantly.

Let them not hate in me,
these three ;
Maid
of the luminous grey-eyes,
Mistress
of honey and marble implacable white thighs
and Goddess,
chaste daughter of Zeus,
most beautiful in the skies.

Let them grow side by side in me,
these three ;
violets,
dipped purple in stark Attic light,
rose,
scorched (on Cyprus coast)
ambrosial white
and wild
exquisite hill-crocus
from Arcadian snows.

BIRDS IN SNOW

See,
how they trace
across the very-marble
of this place,
bright sevens and printed fours,
elevens and careful eights,
abracadabra
of a mystic's lore
or symbol
outlined
on a wizard's gate;

like plaques of ancient writ
our garden flags now name
the great and very-great;
our garden flags acclaim
in carven hieroglyph,
here king and kinglet lie,
here prince and lady rest,
mystical queens sleep here
and heroes that are slain

in holy righteous war;
hieratic, slim and fair,
the tracery written here,
proclaims what's left unsaid
in Egypt of her dead.

CHANCE

Chance says,
come here,
chance says,
can you bear

to part ?
chance says,
sweetheart,
we haven't loved

for almost a year,
can you bear
this loneliness ?
I can't ;

apart from you,
I fear
wind,
bird,

sea,
wave,
low places
and the high air ;

I hear
dire threat
everywhere ;
I start

at wind
in sycamores,
I can't bear
anything

further ;
chance says,
dear,
I 'm here,

don't you want me
any more ?

WHEN I AM A CUP

When I am a cup
lifted up,
can you hear
echo in a seashell?

> *When you are a cup*
> *there is no sigh nor song,*
> *only the weed, the weed,*
> *trailing along.*

When I am a cup
made of shell,
O, can you hear
distant, ringing sea-bells?

> *When you are a cup*
> *there is no sound,*
> *but of seaweed trailing*
> *across sandy ground.*

SIGIL

I

Ground
under a maple-tree
breeds parasite,

so I
bear tentacles, as it were,
from you, tree-loam ;

ground
under a beach
breeds faun-lily, each

tree
spreads separate leaf-mould,
whether maple or beach,

whether paper-birch ;
I come
as those parasites

out of frost almost,
Indian-pipe, hypatica
or the spotted snake-cup,

adder-root, blood-root,
or the white, white plaque
of the wild dog-wood tree ;

each alone,
each separately, I come
separate parasite,

white spear-head
with implacable fragile shoot
from black loam.

II

This is my own world,
these can't see ;
I hear, " this is my dower,"

I fear no man, no woman ;
flower does not fear
bird, insect nor adder ;

I fear neither the wind
nor viper,
familiar sound

bids me raise
frost-nipped, furred head
from winter-ground ;

familiar scent
makes me say,
" I am awake " ;

familiar touch
makes me say, " all this was over-done,
much

was wasted, blood and bone spent
toward this last
secret

wild,
wild,
wild fulfilment."

III

For :
I am not man,
I am not woman ;
I crave

you
as the sea-fish
the wave.

IV

When you turn to sleep
and love is over,
I am your own;

when you want to weep
for some never-found lover,
I come;

when you would think,
" what was the use of it,"
you 'll remember

something you can't grasp
and you 'll wonder
what it was

altered your mood;
suddenly, summer grass
and clover

will be spread,
and you 'll whisper,
" I 've forgotten something,

what was it,
what was it,
I wanted to remember ? "

V

That will be me,
silver
and wild and free;

that will be me
to send a shudder through you,
cold wind

through an aspen tree;
that will be me
to bid you recover

every voice,
every sound,
every syllable

from grass-blade,
tree-toad,
from every wisp and feather

of fern
and moss
and grass,

from every wind-flower,
tethered
by a thread,

from every thread-stem
and every thread-root
and acorns half-broken

above ground
and under the ground.

VI

Confine
your measure to the boundary of the sky,
take all that, I

am quite content
with fire-fly,
with butter-fly ;

take everything,
I compensate my soul
with a new rôle ;

you 're free
but you 're only a song,
I 'm free but I 've gone ;

I 'm not here,
being everywhere
you are.

VII

Whether this happened before,
whether this happen again,
it 's the same ;

there is no magic nor lure,
there is no spell and no power
to equalise love's fire ;

whether he fasten his car
with the bright doves and afar
threaten great Zeus and the stars ;

or whether he cringe at my feet,
whether he beat on your eyes,
white wings, white butterflies.

EPITAPH

So I may say,
" I died of living,
having lived one hour " ;

so they may say,
" she died soliciting
illicit fervour " ;

so you may say,
" Greek flower ; Greek ecstasy
reclaims for ever

one who died
following
intricate songs' lost measure."

THE MYSTERIES

Renaissance Choros

Dark
days are past
and darker days draw near ;
darkness on this side,
darkness over there
threatens the spirit
like massed hosts
a sheer
handful
of thrice-doomed spearsmen ;
enemy this side,
enemy a part
of hill
and mountain-crest
and under-hill ;
nothing before of mystery,
nothing past,
only the emptiness,
pitfall of death,
terror,
the flood,
the earthquake,
stormy ill ;
then voice within the turmoil,
that slight breath
that tells as one flower may
of winter past
(that kills

with Pythian bow,
the Delphic pest ;)
one flower,
slight voice,
reveals
all holiness
with
" peace
be still."

II

A sceptre
and a flower-shaft
and a spear,
one flower may kill the winter,
so this rare
enchanter
and magician
and arch-mage;
one flower may slay the winter
and meet death,
so this
goes and returns
and dies
and comes to bless
again,
again;
a sceptre and a flower
and a near
protector
to the lost and impotent;
yea,
I am lost,
behold what star is near;
yea,
I am weak,
see
what enchanted armour
clothes the intrepid mind
that sheds the gear
of blighting thought;

behold what wit is here
what subtlety,
what humour
and what light ;
see,
I am done,
no lover and none dear,
a voice within the fever,
that slight breath
belies our terror
and our hopelessness,
" lo,
I am here."

III

" Not to destroy,
nay, but to sanctify
the flower
that springs
Adonis
from the dead ;
behold,
behold
the lilies
how they grow,
behold how fair,
behold how pure a red,
(so love has died)
behold the lilies
bled
for love ;
not emperor nor ruler,
none may claim
such splendour ;
king may never boast
so beautiful a garment
as the host
of field
and mountain lilies."

IV

" Not to destroy,
nay, but to sanctify
each flame
that springs
upon the brow of Love ;
not to destroy
but to re-invoke
and name
afresh each flower,
serpent
and bee
and bird ;
behold,
behold
the spotted snake
how wise ;
behold the dove,
the sparrow,
not one dies
without your father ;
man sets the trap
and bids the arrow fly,
man snares the mother-bird
while passing by
the shivering fledglings,
leaving them to lie
starving ;
no man,
no man,
no man

may ever fear
that this one,
winnowing the lovely air,
is overtaken by a bird of prey,
that this is stricken
in its wild-wood plight,
that this dies broken
in the wild-wood snare,
I
and my father
care."

V

" Not to destroy,
nay, but to sanctify
the fervour
of all ancient mysteries ;
behold the dead are lost,
the grass has lain
trampled
and stained
and sodden ;
behold,
behold,
behold
the grass disdains
the rivulet
of snow and mud and rain ;
the grass,
the grass
rises
with flower-bud ;
the grain
lifts its bright spear-head
to the sun again ;
behold,
behold
the dead
are no more dead,
the grain is gold,
blade,
stalk
and seed within ;

the mysteries
are in the grass
and rain."

VI

" The mysteries remain,
I keep the same
cycle of seed-time
and of sun and rain ;
Demeter in the grass
I multiply,
renew and bless
Iacchus in the vine ;
I hold the law,
I keep the mysteries true,
the first of these
to name the living, dead ;
I am red wine and bread.

I keep the law,
I hold the mysteries true,
I am the vine,
the branches, you
and you."